PRINCIPAL PARTS of a

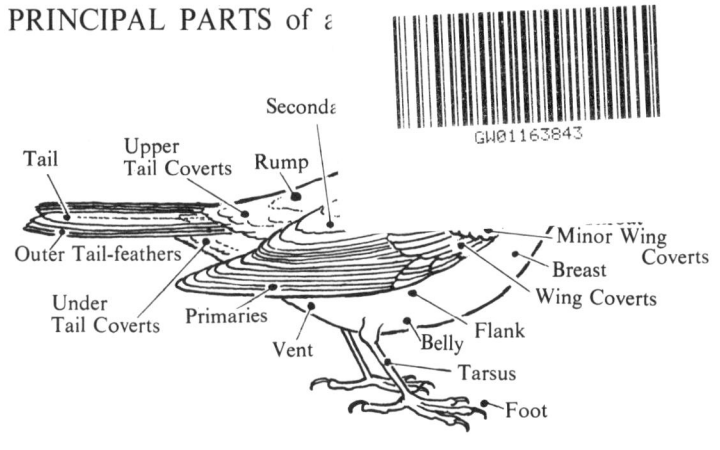

A FEATHER

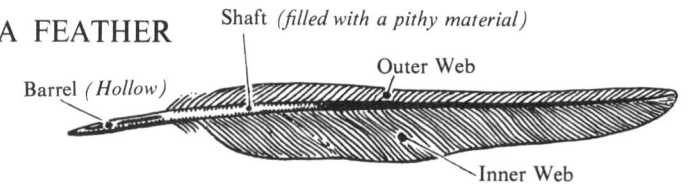

The Barrel and Shaft together are called the Quill

A WING

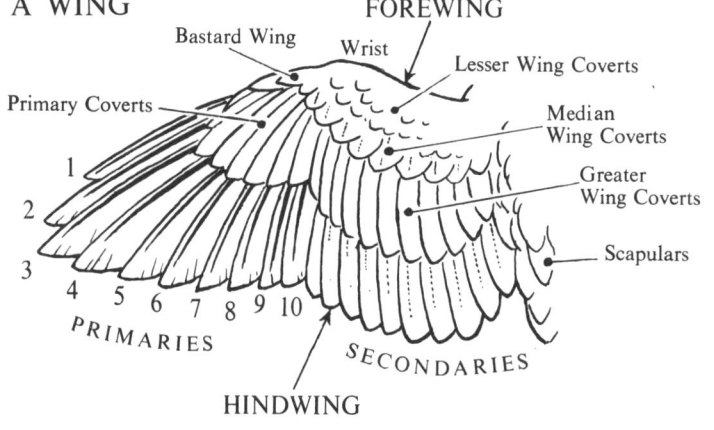

A Ladybird Nature Book
Series 536

It is probably true to say that everyone is interested in birds at some time. This book is planned to help those children — and adults — who have noticed birds in or near their garden and have wished to identify them more positively.

The superb colour illustrations by John Leigh-Pemberton will make identification easy, and the clear, interesting and reliable text will certainly stimulate many people to take an even greater interest in the fascinating subject of bird life.

GARDEN BIRDS

by JOHN LEIGH-PEMBERTON

Publishers: Ladybird Books Ltd . Loughborough
© Ladybird Books Ltd (formerly Wills & Hepworth Ltd) 1967
Printed in England

Green Woodpecker *(left)*
Great Spotted Woodpeckers *(right)*

Woodpeckers live on insects for which they search the trunks and branches of trees. For this purpose they have specially powerful toes, two facing forward and two back, and stiff, pointed tail feathers which act as a prop as they climb, always from the bottom of the tree upwards. They also have extremely long tongues. As they search they tap with their bills, and Great Spotted Woodpeckers in particular do this in the breeding season, making a very loud 'drumming' noise. Woodpeckers bore holes in tree trunks to make their nests, which are unlined. Both species lay four to seven eggs. Only one family is raised, and this is fed by both parents.

Easily recognised, Woodpeckers are fairly common and live in Britain all the year round. There is no real song, but Green Woodpeckers make a loud, laughing cry, and Great Spotted Woodpeckers a harsh 'tchick-tchick.' The Green Woodpecker is the one most often seen in gardens; as well as being bigger and brightly coloured, it is more inclined than other members of the family to appear boldly in the open, searching a lawn for ants.

Magpie *(above)*
Jay *(below)*

Both these birds are members of the Crow family and are exceptionally intelligent, being able to learn from experience and observation.

Magpies eat almost anything and collect and hoard food and sometimes brightly coloured or shining objects. They are present in Britain throughout the year, usually in pairs or in small parties, and in April lay from five to eight eggs in a large nest. This is often placed high in a tree and lined first with earth, then with fine roots. Over it a sort of dome of thorny sticks is built. Magpies utter a loud chattering cry, but can make many other sounds as well.

Jays, too, are capable of all sorts of cries but the most usual is a loud screech, repeated twice and nearly always answered at once by another Jay. They are good mimics and will imitate other birds and animals and even man-made noises. Jays are usually found not far from oak trees, for their diet contains a great many acorns as well as insects, young birds and animals. Four to six eggs, very variable in colour, are laid in a nest of twigs and earth, lined with fibrous roots and usually built fairly low down in bushes or small trees.

Swift (top)

House Martin *(centre)*

Swallow *(right)*

Swallows and House Martins are aerial birds, eating and drinking in flight and only occasionally settling on the ground to collect nesting material. The nests of both species are often placed on buildings and made of mud, held together by pieces of grass or straw and lined with feathers. Swallows nest on ledges and House Martins under the eaves. Both lay four or five eggs and have two broods a year. Their food consists of insects taken on the wing at varying heights and with amazing agility. Swallows have a musical twittering song, while House Martins are quieter and more 'chirrupping'.

Swifts are not related to Swallows and House Martins but they look and behave rather alike. Their immensely long wings and short legs make settling on the ground almost impossible, and even nesting material is picked up in flight; this consists of all sorts of matter which is bound together with the bird's saliva to build a nest in a crevice or under the eaves of a house. Two or three white eggs are laid and there is only one brood. Swifts make a characteristic screaming cry when in flight.

All three birds come to us in spring, returning to Africa between July and October. The Swift is the first to go.

Carrion Crow

Crows are large birds, usually seen alone or in pairs, and although they are found in many different kinds of country, including the sea shore, they regularly visit gardens, even in towns, in order to pick up scraps of food. They eat almost anything, from small animals and birds to insects and seeds, and chiefly feed on the ground where they walk or hop with an amusing action rather like dancing. Food with a hard shell, such as nuts; shellfish or snails, is carried to a height and then dropped, the crow following it down to where it breaks open on the ground. This is but one of the many indications of this bird's unusual intelligence.

The Carrion Crow is a common resident in England and Wales. In the north of Scotland and Ireland it is replaced by another race, the grey-bodied Hooded Crow. The nest is large, nearly always in the fork of a tree, made of sticks, twigs, earth and moss and thickly lined with wool and hair. There are four or five eggs which are hatched by the hen only, although both parents build the nest and feed the young.

The chief cry is a deep, harsh 'Kraak' but crows also screech when angry, or utter a horn-like 'Konk'.

Long-tailed Tit *(top)*

Coal Tit *(left)*

Blue Tit *(right)*

Tits, small dumpy birds with short bills, usually live in flocks or family parties and all eat insects, fruit and seeds.

Long-tailed Tits sometimes make brief visits to gardens, normally in a busy flock; but as a rule they live and breed in woodland and are found throughout the year in most parts of Britain. Their nest is a remarkable, domed structure built of moss, hair and cobwebs with an entrance hole near the top; it is covered with lichen and lined with more than a thousand feathers. Up to twelve eggs are laid, sometimes as early as the end of March. There is no song but a little call—'tsee-tsee'.

The Coal Tit is distinguishable by the white patch behind the head. It climbs up tree trunks, rather like a Treecreeper, and is bold, acrobatic and inquisitive, as all tits are. Its song is a quite powerful 'cher-tee cher-tee' and the call is a thin 'zee'.

The Blue Tit, one of the commonest garden birds, raises a large family of up to fifteen chicks; there is usually only one brood. The nest is placed in a hole of some kind and nesting boxes are frequently used. There is a shrill little trill of a song and a scolding call: 'tsee-tsee-tsit'.

Wren *(above)*
Great Tit *(below)*

The Wren is resident in all parts of the British Isles and can be seen throughout the year. This tiny, mouse-like bird prefers the cover of banks and bushes. Its usual note is a rapid 'tic-tic-tic', but it also sings a shrill, clear song, very loud indeed for such a small bird; sometimes it sings while making its short, straight and rapid flight. In spring, the cock-bird builds several unlined nests which are domed and have an entrance at the side. The hen chooses one, lines it with feathers and lays from four to six tiny eggs which are white, speckled with red. There are usually two broods.

The Great Tit is found in most gardens; it is very intelligent and bold, quickly becoming tame. It eats insects and seeds, fruit buds or worms, and holds its food down with a foot while eating. The nest is built in a hole in a wall or tree or often in nest-boxes. From five to eleven eggs are laid, and the young are raised by both parents; one brood is usual. Great Tits have many different notes, from an angry hiss to 'tee-chu, tee-chu', repeated over and over again, which is the commonest song.

Nuthatch *(top)*
Treecreeper *(below)*

Both these birds live mostly on the trunks and limbs of trees, finding there the insects upon which they feed. They are resident birds and are fairly common in the British Isles, although the Nuthatch, which also eats berries and acorns, is not found in Scotland or Ireland and is rare in western and northern England. Their methods of working over a tree differ; the Treecreeper flies to the bottom of a tree and, working upwards, propped on its pointed tail feathers, moves jerkily and in a spiral round the trunk; the Nuthatch moves in any direction in a series of little jumps, often working head downwards. The Nuthatch appears more often in the open and will feed from a bird table, sometimes hiding the food it takes, but the Treecreeper is shy and less readily seen.

The Treecreeper usually builds its narrow nest of twigs and chips, with a soft lining, under a loose piece of bark or in a crevice. The Nuthatch chooses a hole and reduces the size of the entrance by partially filling it with mud. Each lays from four to eight eggs.

The Nuthatch has a great variety of calls, including a low 'chwit-chwit', and a high-pitched trill. Treecreepers make a weak little "tsee" sound and, often when climbing, sing a rather squeaky song with a hurried trill at the end.

Robin *(above)*

Dunnock *(below)*

The Robin is a member of the Thrush family, a bird for which a garden, with its thick cover and varied diet of worms and insects, is particularly suitable. Very bold and tame, Robins, like many birds, have 'territories' from about half to two acres in extent, but varying in size according to numbers. Both cock and hen Robins look alike, and sing nearly all the year round—a clear, melodious warble often heard also at night. There is a scolding 'tic-tic' and a high-pitched 'tzee' in the breeding season. The well-built nest is found in odd places—in sheds and old cans as well as the more normal hedge or bush. There are from four to six eggs and usually two broods.

The Dunnock is sometimes quite wrongly called the Hedge Sparrow. It is really an 'accentor' and not a sparrow at all. Like the Robin, it feeds largely on the ground on insects but also takes seeds; it is a most melodious all-the-year-round singer. This dainty little bird is often overlooked, as it spends much time in cover. The hen builds a very neat nest well concealed in a thick bush, and lays from four to six beautiful, blue eggs. There are two or even three broods.

Blackbird (cock above, hen below)

Blackbirds are members of the Thrush family and are with us all the year throughout the British Isles. In both summer and winter there are also visiting blackbirds from Europe. This very common bird is one of our finest songsters, and has a fluty, melodious song which is full of variety. There is also the often-heard alarm note—a sudden piercing rattle, 'tac-tac-tac', and the quieter 'chuck-chuck', almost like a conversation. Blackbirds eat worms, insects, fruit and seeds, spending much time foraging upon the ground, but frequently flying off, close to the ground, either to cover or to some vantage point where the tail is flicked gracefully up and down.

The nest is built by the hen, though the site is sometimes chosen by the cock; it is usually placed in a bush (ivy is very popular), but can be in a tree and even on the ground. It is well made and can be distinguished from the very similar Song Thrush's nest by its inner lining of dried grass. There are normally three to five eggs, and these are hatched by the hen alone. The young birds are like the hen but more spotted, and there are two or more broods. Blackbirds, especially cocks, often have some white feathers, and all-white birds are not very unusual.

Song Thrush (above)
Redwing (below)

All over Britain the Song Thrush is a resident bird which seems to have a preference for gardens and houses. It feeds on worms, insects and berries. Its feeding methods are interesting to watch when it stands motionless, listening for the movement of a worm or insect, or when it takes a snail and hammers the shell upon a stone. Not as noisy as the Blackbird, its song is even more melodious, being very clear and precise; 'Did-he-do-it? He-did-he-did-he-did', gives a fair idea of the song. The nest is made of twigs, moss or grass and is lined smooth with rotten wood, mud or dung. Three to five eggs are laid and there are two broods, sometimes more.

The Redwing is another sort of Thrush which is a winter visitor to this country. It is a pretty bird, notable for the red flanks and under-wings. It eats much the same food as other Thrushes and in winter is particularly fond of berries. A very few Redwings nest in Scotland, but most breed in more northern countries. In this country it sometimes sings before migrating in spring, and appears in our gardens only in hard weather; then it appreciates broken up apples and, like all birds, drinking water.

Black Redstart *(hen above, cock below)*

The Black Redstart is well-known in Europe, on farms, in towns, and also in rocky or mountainous country. In Britain it prefers to nest among habitations, especially ruins. Not so long ago this bird was a scarce winter visitor, chiefly to our south and east coasts, but during and after the war it nested in bombed areas, especially in London. It now nests regularly in this country, and is seen in winter and on passage. The Black Redstart is more likely to be seen in town or seaside gardens than in the country. Its food is chiefly insects, taken on the ground, but sometimes it catches them on the wing, hovering in order to do so; in winter it eats berries.

The nest is in a crevice in a building or cliff, loosely built of mixed materials. The four to six eggs are white and, as with many small birds, take from twelve to fourteen days to hatch. Usually there are two broods. This is another member of the Thrush family, with a rather plaintive call-note and a loud 'tucc-tucc' of alarm. The song is peculiar; it is a soft, rapid warble which suddenly stops and gives way to an odd, metallic rattling sound.

Starling *(above)*
Mistle Thrush *(below)*

Generally, the Starling is a resident bird but huge flocks from the north of Europe visit us in winter. This is a busy, noisy bird which, because of its numbers, can become a pest in both town and country; but, closely examined, its plumage is remarkably beautiful. The most spectacular thing about it, however, is the range of its voice, not only its own clicking and whistling but also its imitation of the songs and calls of many other birds. Starlings nest in crevices and lay four to six pale blue eggs, often at odd times of the year, and there is usually one brood only.

The Mistle Thrush is the biggest of our British Thrushes and can be distinguished from the Song Thrush by being larger, greyer and more boldly spotted. It is with us all the year round but appears in gardens mostly in the breeding season. The Mistle Thrush spends a lot of time on the ground, standing up very straight, and feeding on worms and insects and on fruit and berries. When it sings, it perches high up and the song is short, loud and 'fluty'. It flies higher, and nests higher, than other thrushes, building a large, unconcealed nest and laying three to five eggs, which it defends most bravely. There are two broods.

Garden Warbler (top)
Blackcap (hen above, cock below)

These Warblers are summer visitors and woodland birds which occasionally visit large gardens where there is plenty of thick cover. Although rather alike in feeding and nesting habits, they seem to avoid each other, and are not likely to be found in the same garden. Both build light, grassy nests in low bushes or hedgerows and raise families of four or five, sometimes with two broods. The Garden Warbler cock builds 'cock nests' in the same way that a Wren does.

The song of both birds, especially the Blackcap, is outstanding. The Garden Warbler will sing its low-pitched warble without interruption for minutes on end, although the bird itself is nearly always hidden in a bush while doing so. The Blackcap's song is sweeter, higher and shorter, and has been described as sounding like 'hee-ti-weeto-weeto'. When they first arrive, in April, Blackcaps seem to be 'practising' their song very quietly; after a few days they sing with full power. The songs of these two birds are sometimes difficult to tell apart, as each is capable of imitating the other.

By October, both birds have left us for Southern Europe and North Africa, but a few Blackcaps winter in Britain; these are probably visitors from Europe.

Willow Warbler (above)
Chiffchaff (below)

These little birds, both fairly common in gardens, are what is known as 'leaf-warblers', so called because their small size, shape, and general colour is very like a leaf.

They are difficult to tell apart—the chief difference is in the song. The Willow Warbler will sing continuously, a succession of rippling notes descending the scale; the Chiffchaff will go on all day, endlessly repeating the two notes 'chiff-chaff' from which it gets it's name. In appearance the Willow Warbler is a little greener above and yellower below than the Chiffchaff, which is more inclined to be buffish; and generally the Willow Warbler has pale legs, whereas those of the Chiffchaff are usually dark.

Both are summer visitors, arriving in March and leaving in September or October, but a few of each species winter here. Willow Warblers nest on the ground or near it, but the Chiffchaff builds higher, sometimes in thick evergreens such as holly bushes. Both lay six or seven eggs and sometimes have two broods in the south. Like other warblers they are principally insect eaters, especially in spring and summer when there are young to feed, but they will eat berries in the autumn.

Spotted Flycatcher *(above)*
Pied Flycatcher *(cock left, hen right)*

Flycatchers are summer visitors, arriving rather late in Spring, and they get their name from their feeding habits. They will sit on some vantage point, such as a post, and will wait for insects to come close; they then dart out and catch them, usually in the air.

Spotted Flycatchers are found nearly all over Britain and are frequently seen in gardens, for they are quite happy to nest in garden sheds or on the beam of a house. The nest is rather flimsy, made of moss, wool and cobwebs, and about five young, much more spotted than their parents, are raised. There is hardly any song, just a squeaky phrase which is easy to miss. The most interesting thing about the Spotted Flycatcher is its method of feeding and its acrobatic, dancing flight as it does so.

The Pied Flycatcher is smaller and rarer and is found chiefly in the north and west of Britain. It is a much better songster: 'tchee-tchee-tchee-cher-cher' with variations, but the song period is short. It nests in holes of trees, sometimes in buildings and often in nesting boxes, raising as many as nine young in the single brood. It is more inclined than the Spotted Flycatcher to feed on the ground, where it catches spiders.

House Sparrow *(top; hen above, cock below)*
Pied Wagtail *(below)*

Wherever there are human dwellings there are almost certain to be House Sparrows, but they are not to be found in wild places at all. They frequently build their nests on houses, fairly high up and often in groups. Usually they keep the same mate for life, and return every year to the same nesting place. Here they may raise three broods of from three to five eggs in the clutch, the type of nest varying according to where it is placed; it is bulky in trees but may be quite small in the hole of a wall. Although they are noisy and quarrelsome, Sparrows have no real song, but make a continuous cheeping noise. They eat almost anything and can survive the severest conditions.

The Pied Wagtail, too, likes to nest near houses, but is also often found near water. This bird is a great eater of insects, catching them either in the air or by running along the ground. Unlike many other small birds it does not hop, but walks, balancing itself with its long tail. The simple, twittering song is not often heard. The nest, usually in some sort of hollow, is stoutly made and well lined; there are five or six eggs, hatched by the hen alone. Later it is a very pretty sight to see both parents catching insects for their family.

Lesser Spotted Woodpecker (above)
Chaffinch (below; cock left, hen right)

The Lesser Spotted or Barred Woodpecker is a resident bird, but is absent from the north of Britain. Rather uncommon and, because of its small size, not often noticed, it will visit gardens with high trees in them. It nests in a branch where the wood is rotten and where it can bore a suitable hole. About five glossy, white eggs are hatched by both parents; there is one brood. The Lesser Spotted 'drums' on wood like the Great Spotted Woodpecker, and almost as powerfully, and has a loud, shrill call 'pee-pee-pee-pee-pee', the same rather unmusical note repeated five times.

The Chaffinch is one of the commonest and most widely distributed British land-birds; it is not only a resident but in winter large flocks arrive in the east and spread northwards. It is a typical finch, with a thick, seed-eating bill and dipping, undulating flight. Busy, bold and perky, the Chaffinch has a pleasant, gay song as well as the usual call: 'chink-chink'. The very neat, mossy nest, usually in a bush, is decorated outside with lichen or even pieces of paper. There is one clutch of four to six eggs. This is a good friend to the gardener, eating great numbers of weed seeds, and destroying many grubs and caterpillars.

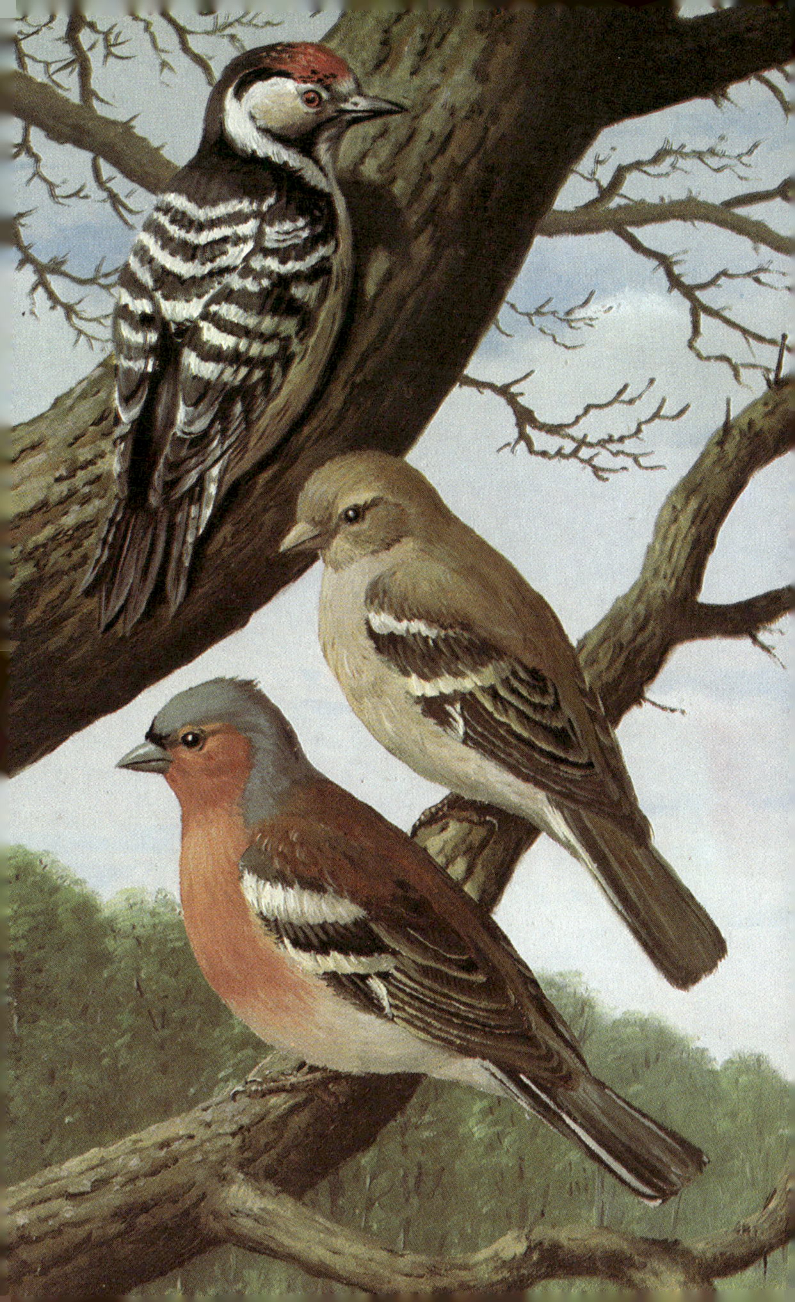

Bullfinch *(hen above, cock below)*

A garden which contains fruit trees is very likely to be visited by Bullfinches; for, although in summer and autumn they will eat berries and insects, in spring they pick and eat great quantities of buds from fruit trees. For this reason they can do a lot of damage. Bullfinches do not mix much with other birds, but are usually found in pairs. For most of the year they are woodland birds, inclined to hide in cover; so that, in spite of their bulky shape and bright colour, they are not often seen. They are resident all over England, but less so in Scotland.

The nest varies; sometimes it is rather flimsy and at others very stout. But the special thing about it is that it is very frequently lined with fine black roots. Four to six greenish-blue speckled eggs are hatched by the hen alone; and there are usually two broods. Both parents feed the young birds, mainly on insects. The young can fly in about fourteen days and spend their first months in a family party.

Bullfinches have an easily recognised cry—a sort of whistled 'deu-deu'. The song is only a low warble, uttered by both cock and hen.

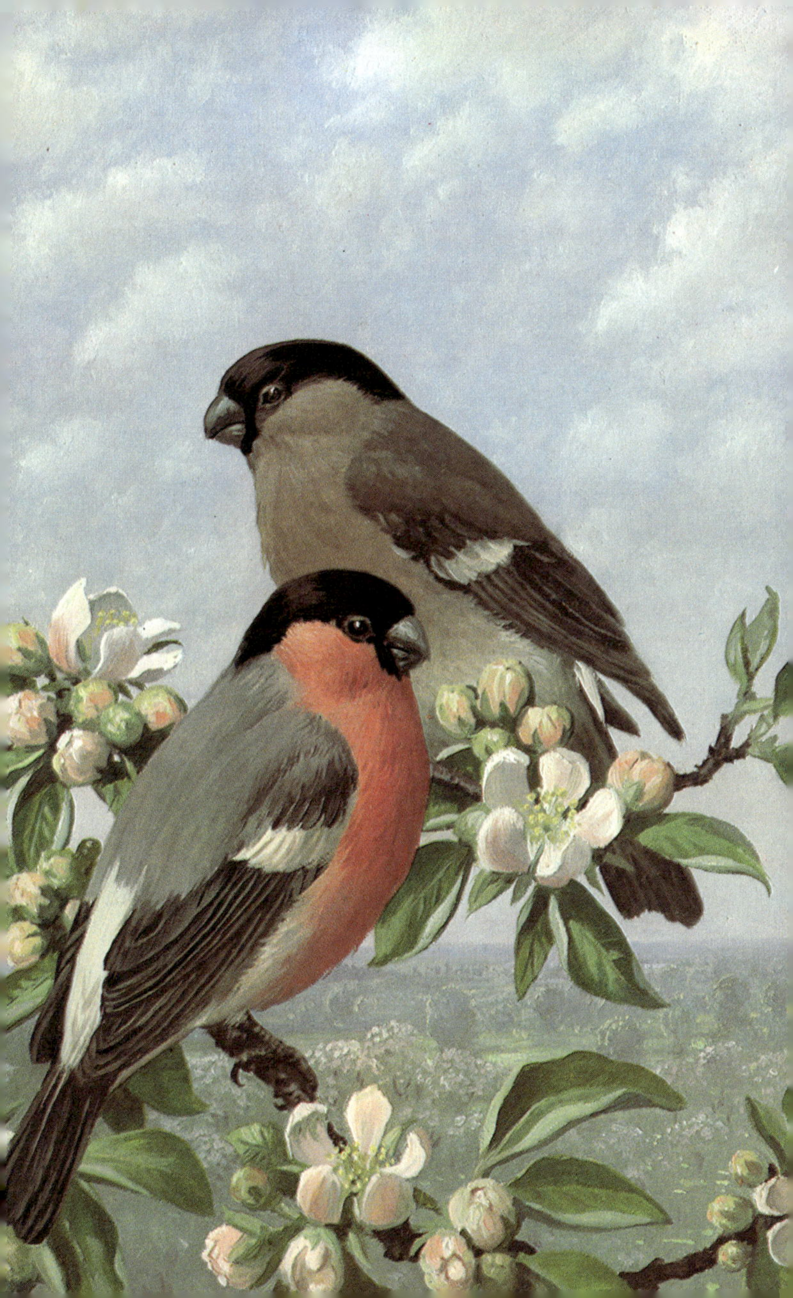

Linnet (cock above, hen below)

Linnets are finches which like country with plenty of thick bushes, particularly gorse; but in the spring they often come to gardens to breed. The cock bird is very pretty in his summer plumage, but in autumn he becomes much more like the hen; and this change in plumage is the reason why the Linnet has several different names (such as 'Grey Linnet' or 'Red Linnet' or 'Common Linnet') all of which really refer to the same bird. Linnets generally go about in flocks, wheeling and dipping in formation; and they sometimes nest in colonies, when the cocks will sing in chorus. The song is not loud, but it is mostly soft and musical, not unlike a Canary's.

The hen builds the nest by herself, fairly low down in a thick bush or hedge. A variety of materials including hair, grass and wool is used. Four to six eggs can be hatched in as little as ten days and there may be two or three broods. Both parents feed the young.

Linnets are resident birds all over Britain; but in autumn some birds migrate to Southern France, returning the following spring. Other Linnets from the Continent come to us for the winter.

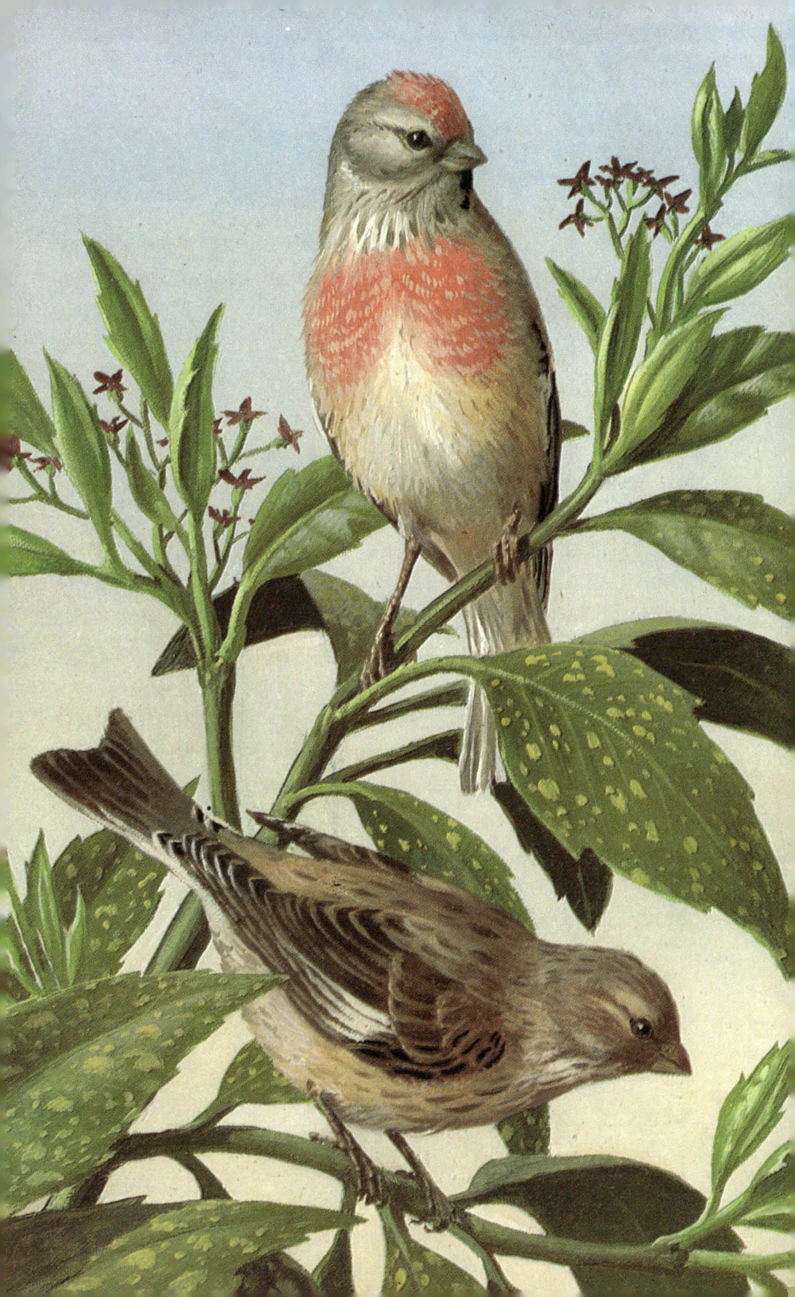

Goldfinch *(above)*

Hawfinch *(below)*

Finches have stout bills specially suitable for eating seeds. The Goldfinch, which is small and dainty, and the Hawfinch, which is thick and heavy, show what a big difference there can be in one 'family'.

Goldfinches are easily recognised and often breed in gardens, raising about five young in a beautiful, neat nest built by the hen. There are at least two broods. As with other seed-eaters, the young are fed on insects alone, although mature birds will include weed seeds, especially thistles, in their diet. The Goldfinch's call is 'twitt-itt-itt' and the song is really a development of this.

Goldfinches are resident, but at one time the Hawfinch was only a rare visitor. During the past hundred years it has gradually become a resident bird, although it is not common, and does not occur at all in some areas. It is a woodland bird, found in gardens only where the trees are tall enough for it to perch in the highest branches. With its huge beak it can even crack cherry stones to reach the kernel.

The nest is shallow, built on a platform of twigs and with a cup of lichen, moss, hair or roots. Four to six eggs are hatched by the hen alone. The song is weak and not often heard, but their sharp call 'tzik', is the best means of detecting Hawfinches.

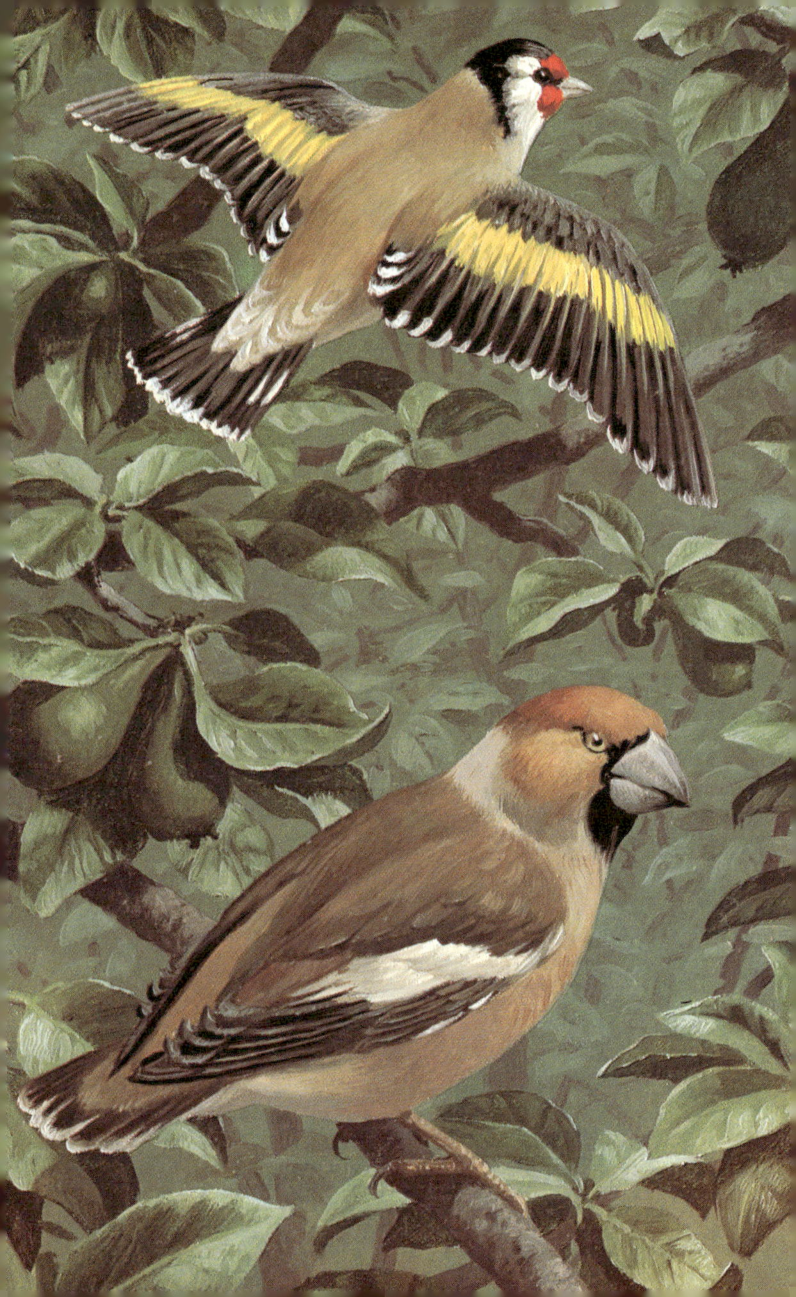

Greenfinch (cock above, hen below)

In the breeding season the Greenfinch is very much of a garden bird, prefering shrubberies to big woods, and several pairs sometimes nest in neighbouring bushes. It is a sociable bird which lives in family parties and large flocks, often mixed with other finches. In winter it is a common visitor to bird-tables and is particularly fond of peanuts.

Greenfinches are easily recognised, for no other greenish bird has the bright yellow bar on the wing. It is mainly a resident, occurring almost everywhere in the British Isles; but visiting Greenfinches come over in large numbers from Northern Europe in autumn.

With its large bill it can manage quite tough food, such as wheat grains and hard berries, and even the young are partly fed on seeds. There are two broods of about five eggs, but, as with many birds, this number can vary a lot, and there may be as many as seven or as few as three eggs.

The Greenfinch's cry is a long, often repeated 'tswee'; but it also has a different note 'chi-chi-chi-chi-chit', uttered in flight, and the call 'tsooeet' like that of many other finches. The song is really a combination of these, and is heard almost throughout the year.

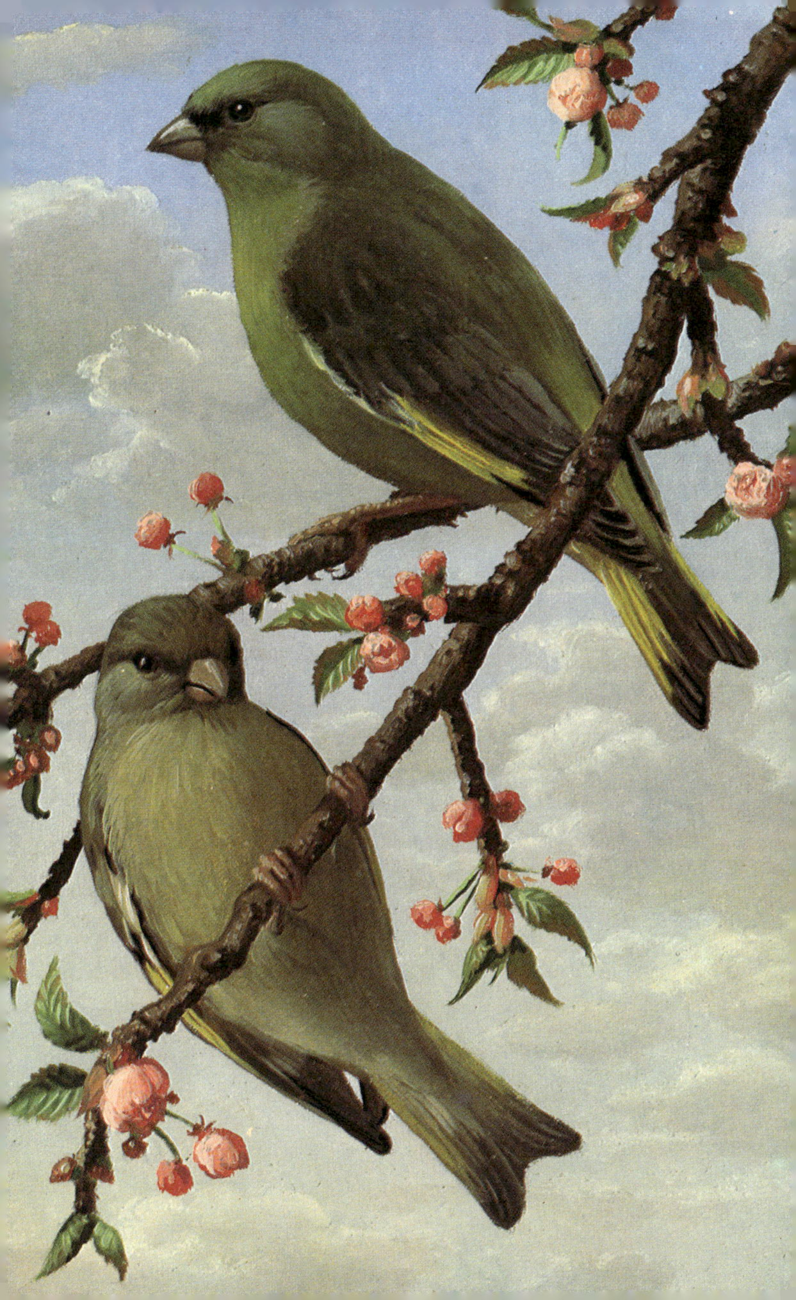

Woodpigeon (above)
Collared Dove (below)

The Woodpigeon was once considered to be a shy bird, belonging strictly to country woodland. But now it is found all over Britain in town parks and in gardens, where it becomes exceedingly tame. It has an enormous appetite, eating mostly vegetable food, often doing great damage to crops. This big bird, sixteen inches long, can always be recognised by the white neck patches and the typical five note song 'coo-cooo-coo coo-coo'. It makes a flat, untidy nest of twigs, built by the hen with material provided by the cock. There may be several broods of two chicks each; these take about eighteen days to hatch from the white eggs and it may be as long as a month before the young fly.

The Collared Dove is a recent newcomer to Britain. It has gradually spread across Europe from Asia Minor and is now breeding here in many places. This pretty little dove likes to live near human dwellings and is further attracted by the food in chicken runs, and by ilex and fir trees. The call (three notes) is distinctive—'coo-cooo-coo'. The nest is scanty, and several broods of two young are raised, the cock sitting by day and the hen at night.

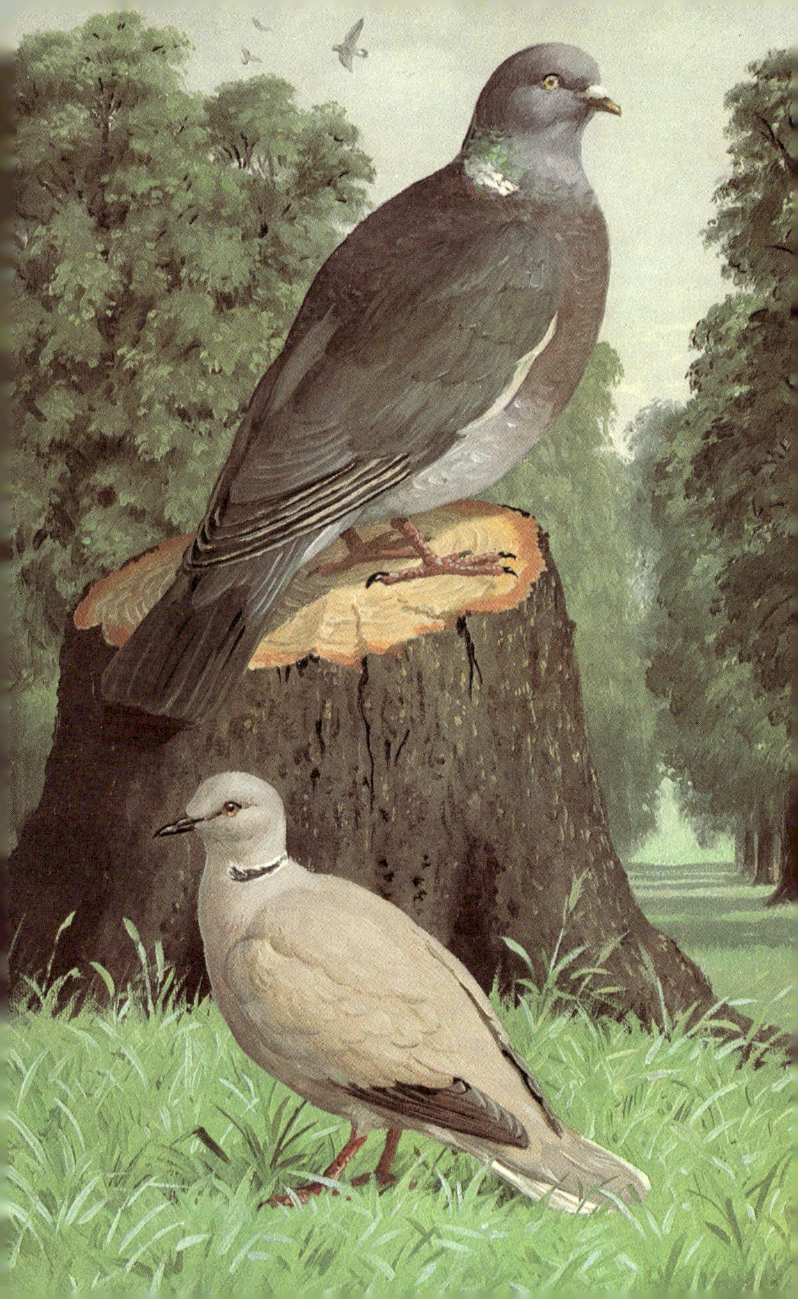

Tawny Owl

Owls hunt by swooping upon their prey from above; their flight is silent and they have wonderful hearing and eyesight. Their ears and flat faces are specially adapted to the way in which they live.

The Tawny Owl is active only at night. In daytime it roosts in a tall tree, close up against the trunk. During the day small birds sometimes gather round a roosting owl to scold and 'mob' it. At dusk it comes out to hunt —mice, voles, small birds, worms and even fish. It is then that the well known cry is heard—'kewick', or the hoot—'hoo-hoo-hoo-hoo'.

This is a resident, found all over Britain (but not in Ireland) and it is a bird particularly fond of buildings, even in towns. It is probably the fiercest British bird, quite ready to defend its nest and young by striking with its formidable talons at the head of even a human intruder. Like all other birds, it should be left in peace.

The nest is most often in a hollow in a tree or building, but may also be on the ground or in a rabbit burrow. There is no nesting material and the number of eggs varies between two and four in one clutch. The young remain with their parents for nearly three months.

Barn Owl

The Barn Owl is not very common but is resident over most of England and Wales. It is scarce in Scotland and Ireland. Towers, hollow trees or farm buildings are the places in which it chooses to live and nest. Although active chiefly at night, this Owl can sometimes be seen in late daylight, particularly when it has a family to feed. It is a good friend to the farmer, for it kills quantities of rats and mice, although its diet includes insects.

Like other owls, its flight is silent, the feathers of the rounded wing being specially formed to make this possible. When roosting, it sits bolt upright, often on one leg. It makes many different and very odd noises; the ordinary call, a long, rather alarming shriek, is often uttered on the wing. But it will also hiss when hungry or anxious, or snap its beak when angry; both adults and young have a loud call which sounds like a human snoring.

There is no nest—just a hollow, or even nothing more than the flat top to a beam or ledge. Three to seven eggs are laid at fairly long intervals, so that a family often consists of several owlets of differing age and size. They are at least two months old before they fly.

INDEX

	Page		Page
Blackbird - - - -	20	Owl (Tawny) - - -	48
Blackcap - - - -	28	Redwing - - - -	22
Black Redstart - - -	24	Robin - - - - -	18
Bullfinch - - - -	38		
		Starling - - - -	26
Carrion Crow - - -	10	Swallow - - - -	8
Chaffinch - - - -	36	Swift - - - - -	8
Chiffchaff - - - -	30		
Collared Dove - - -	46	Thrush (Mistle) - -	26
		Thrush (Song) - -	22
Dunnock - - - -	18	Tit (Blue) - - - -	12
Flycatcher (Pied) - -	32	Tit (Coal) - - - -	12
Flycatcher (Spotted) -	32	Tit (Great) - - - -	14
Goldfinch - - - -	42	Tit (Longtailed) - -	12
Greenfinch - - - -	44	Treecreeper - - -	16
Hawfinch - - - -	42	Wagtail (Pied) - - -	34
House Martin - - -	8	Warbler (Garden) - -	28
House Sparrow - -	34	Warbler (Willow) - -	30
Jay - - - - -	6	Woodpecker (Great Spotted)	4
Linnet - - - - -	40	Woodpecker (Green)	4
Magpie - - - -	6	Woodpecker (Lesser Spotted)	36
Nuthatch - - - -	16	Woodpigeon - - -	46
Owl (Barn) - - - -	50	Wren - - - - -	14